DATE			

TABLETOP THEATRES

by Louise Cochrane

Illustrated by Kate Simunek

Publishers   PLAYS, INC.   Boston

Text © Louise Cochrane 1973

Illustrations © Kate Simunek 1973

Published in Great Britain
by Chatto & Windus Ltd

First American edition published
by Plays, Inc. 1974

Library of Congress Catalog Card Number: 73-8348
ISBN: 0-8238-0155-1

Printed in Great Britain

CONTENTS

For Francesca Sian Lang

And also for all those who helped to test the
ideas:

Rosalind May
Vanessa Dillon
Nicholas Slee
Philip Hill
Anne Fraser
Sarah and Andrew Mitchell
Serena Hares
Adrian and Andrew Joynt
Caroline White

INTRODUCTION Plays can be acted almost anywhere as long as there is a central spot for the actors and a place for people to watch. A model stage and mini puppets can turn a table-top into an excellent theatre. Designs for making four different types of stage are shown in this book. From them you can see how theatres have changed through the ages.

No theatre comes to life until a play is produced, so for each stage you will find a suitable play for puppets which will show you how the stage was used. There are instructions on how to construct the simple puppets, scenery and stage machinery. You can also make costumes for your mini 'actors' from the pictures of the characters in each of the plays. When performing the plays it will be easier if you ask a friend to help you speak the parts and act the puppets.

Mummers' plays are thought to be the oldest plays in English. Mummers were ordinary village people who wore masks and rough costumes. They performed their plays at Christmas or Easter, in the halls of big houses or out of doors.

In the Middle Ages there were other forms of drama, originally produced by the Church to teach people stories from the Bible and the difference between right and wrong. Later some of these were performed away from churches on pageant wagons which went in procession like floats in a carnival. These plays were acted in the cities, and guilds of craftsmen were responsible for different ones. They tried to outdo one another in introducing new and exciting ideas. There was scenery, with a fierce dragon's mouth for the jaws of Hell. There were effects—smoke and fire from beneath the wagon; crashes of thunder and storm noises for the story of Noah. Elaborate and fancy costumes were made for some characters and comic turns were introduced to keep people amused.

When printing was invented, the rapid spread of learning meant an increased interest in acting at Court. Noble families arranged lavish entertainments for royal visits. The men who could write plays were kept very busy. They drew their ideas not only from the Bible, but from earlier Greek and Roman plays, from ancient legends, from history, and from romantic tales handed down by minstrels and troubadours. People with a talent for acting now found they could make a living by forming themselves into travelling groups. Some regular places for plays to be given were needed. The yards of inns provided an answer for a time, but it was hard to collect enough money to mount the sort of plays people enjoyed. By now English audiences expected the rich costumes and expensive effects which merchants or nobles had previously paid for. There was another problem, too, for the actors. Some plays were a little wild and part of the public strongly disapproved of them. When groups of players had to be sponsored and licensed, it became necessary for them to have proper theatres where people would pay to go and see a play.

Finally, in the first Queen Elizabeth's reign, *The Theatre* was built. That was its name and, for a time, it was the only one. Soon, of course, there were others, like the famous *Globe* where many of Shakespeare's plays were acted. The builders of these theatres knew what the audience had liked when they had watched performances on the pageant wagons or in big houses, or the yards of inns, and this accounts for the way in which the Elizabethan stage—our first model—was built. **5**

CHAPTER 1   The Elizabethan Stage

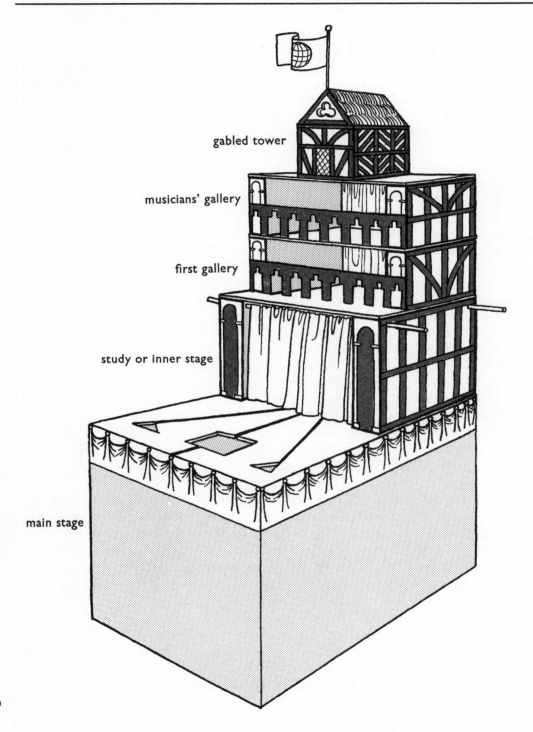

gabled tower

musicians' gallery

first gallery

study or inner stage

main stage

what you need

★ Newspaper to cover your working surface.

★ Large, sharp, cutting-out scissors.

★ A pencil and ruler.

★ Poster paints, crayons or felt pens.

★ Sellotape or glue paste. (If you use paste, buy a small packet of wallpaper paste and mix a teaspoonful of granules at a time in a saucer of water.)

★ Paper-clips or clothes-pegs; drawing-pins.

for making the stage and its machinery

★ A cardboard grocery carton about 50 cm by 30 cm by 20 cm.

★ Six smaller cardboard boxes; two of the same size (about 16 cm by 12 cm) and four slightly smaller and, if possible, identical boxes. Lids and bases of the same boxes can be used in pairs.

★ One small box for the gabled tower.

★ Cardboard, stiff paper and silver paper.

★ Small pieces of material for making three pairs of stage curtains.

★ Rods, long enough to go across the stage and hold the curtains (you may be able to make the rods from straight twigs). Small garden stakes or potting rods would also be suitable.

★ Empty cotton reels; a cardboard tube; a tin tray.

MAKING THE MAIN STAGE

1. Lay newspaper on your working surface. Place the grocery box on the newspaper, open side down.

Mark a rectangle in one of the short sides and cut out as in the diagram. It should be large enough to put your hand and arm through.

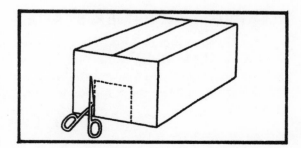

2. If the long flaps on top are held down by fastenings, remove them with the help of a screwdriver or metal nail-file. Open out and cut off the short flaps underneath.

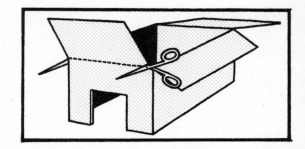

3. Make cuts in the long flaps where indicated at **a**. These are tracks for moving the puppets and should be about 1 cm wide. The diagram shows the main stage looked at from above.

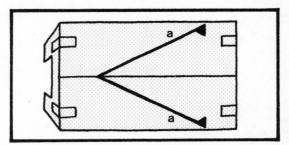

4. Cut out the sections marked **b** and **c**. These are the 'trapdoors'.
5. Make two small holes for the cotton-reel handles.
6. Refasten the long flaps with Sello-tape or strips of paper and paste.

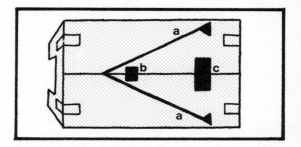

The main stage now has two openings, the 'trapdoors'; and tracks along which the puppets can be moved from underneath. This stage is the most important part of the Elizabethan theatre. The front and sides of it were open and the trapdoors were used for sudden magical appearances of characters. At the back of the main stage there were galleries. Underneath the first gallery was the inner stage called 'the study'. It was curtained off and used for a throne-room, a cave, or any inside scene.

MAKING THE INNER STAGE

1. Use the two larger identical boxes or the lid and base of the same box. Make holes in the long sides where indicated in the diagram. These are for rods to hold curtains.

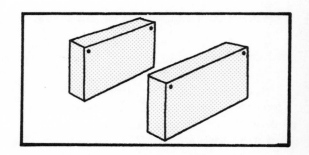

2. Take a piece of material a little wider than the main stage, and the height of the boxes. Cut it in half and pin each curtain to a straight twig or rod. These are the front curtains.

3. Do the same for the back curtains.

4. Place the rods in the holes at each side, front and back. To open your curtains, roll them up around the rods.

5. Cover the inner stage with a piece of cardboard to make a floor for the next gallery. Secure to the boxes with Sellotape or paste.

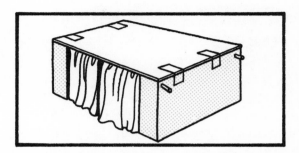

Above the inner stage, and set back a little, was the first gallery. It was used for balcony scenes, city walls, or when a character appeared above the main stage.

MAKING THE FIRST GALLERY

1. Use two of the smaller boxes—or the lid and base of the same box—for the sides of this gallery.

2. Find a piece of cardboard long enough to join the two boxes for a balcony.

3. Cut it to look like railings.

4. Fix in position between the boxes with Sellotape or paste.

5. Cover this stage with a piece of cardboard as before, to make the floor for the musicians' gallery. Secure it to the boxes.

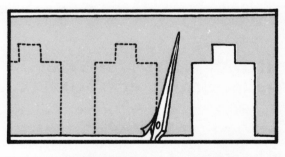

MAKING THE MUSICIANS' GALLERY

1. Follow instructions 1–4 for the making of the first gallery.

2. Place another piece of cardboard over the upper gallery and fasten with Sellotape or paste to the side boxes.

9

3. Make two curtains long enough to hang down behind *both* the musicians' gallery and the first gallery.

4. Fasten the curtains in position by fixing to a rod, and push the rod through the holes as in the diagram.

The puppets make their entrances through these curtains.

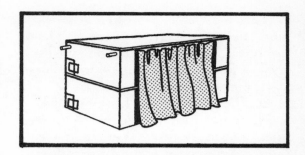

MAKING THE GABLED TOWER

1. Use the small box for the base.
2. Fold a piece of cardboard to fit over the box as a roof.
3. Cut two triangles for gable ends.
4. Secure gable ends and roof to box with Sellotape.

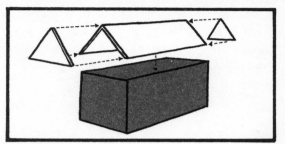

The separate sections are now ready for fastening to the main stage. Use paste and/or Sellotape to secure each section firmly to the one below. If necessary put pebbles in the boxes to weight them. Then the whole building can be painted or coloured. The roof should look as if it is thatched. Make a small flag for the top.

You will not want to cut off the view of your tabletop stage when you are giving a play, so there is no point in making the covered galleries, in which people sat, and which enclosed the main stage. Another important feature of the Elizabethan theatre was that daylight was the main source of light. This was the reason why the pit, or central part, was open to the sky. It was cheaper to sit here, but the audience was also exposed to the weather!

MERLIN PLAYS MINSTREL
MAKING PAPER ROD–PUPPETS

The paper rod-puppets are moved along the tracks from underneath the stage or appear through the curtains from behind.

what you need

★ Thick paper or thin cardboard.
★ Pipe-cleaners or dried flower stalks.
★ Drinking-straws.
★ A needle or pair of compasses; pins.
★ Crayons or felt pens.

what you do

The pattern for Merlin will show you how to make the other puppets. Some face sideways and some forwards, according to how they are moved in the play.

1. Make the puppet in one piece by folding the paper or thin cardboard in half and drawing the outline of Merlin as in the picture.

2. Cut round the outline then open out.

3. Fold along the dotted lines. This will form the base of the puppet.

4. With a needle or compass-point, gently make a hole in the base section.

5. Draw in the face of the puppet on the front. Copy the hat and costume from the picture on back and front and colour brightly.

6. Push a pipe-cleaner up through the base hole to reach the head of the puppet.

7. Pin the back and front of the puppet's head together by pushing a pin downwards; it should also secure the pipe-cleaner.

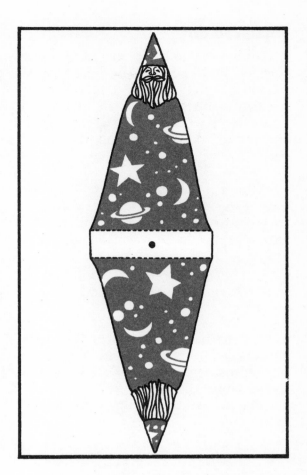

8. Puppets appearing on galleries need to be operated from behind rather than underneath the stage. For these, bend back the pipe-cleaner at base.

MAKING ROLLER PUPPETS
(*suitable for a group of workmen*)

what you need

★ A long strip of paper the height of a cotton reel.

★ Two empty cotton reels.

★ Two sticks, twigs, or pencils to fit in cotton reels for use as handles.

★ Drawing-pins or Sellotape to fasten the strip of paper to the cotton reels.

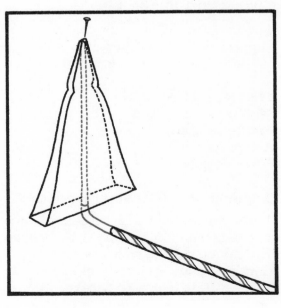

what you do

1. Draw and colour a group of workmen on both sides of the long strip of paper.

2. Attach the left end of the strip to the cotton reel with a drawing-pin. Wind the rest of the strip round the cotton reel.

3. Attach a cotton thread to the right end of the strip, then fasten this thread to the second cotton reel, leaving enough space in between the two reels.

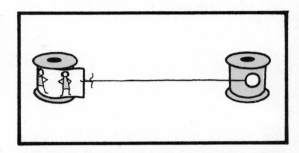

4. Put the handles in place. When the cotton-reel rollers are fixed in position on the stage you can make a procession move from one spot to another by turning the stick handles from underneath.

Characters in the play

The following characters appear in 'Merlin Plays Minstrel'. Those marked * are puppets which face forwards and appear on the galleries. You can copy their costumes from the pictures.

Merlin as a Magician*
Merlin as a Minstrel
Merlin as a Boy
Arthur as a Boy
King Vortigern*

Two Workmen
Court Adviser*
A Guard
Red Dragon
White Dragon

Scenery and Machinery needed

A tower made out of a cardboard tube or plastic container. This is pushed up through one of the trapdoors.
Dark material for curtains of inner stage to make this look like a cave.

Silver paper to give the idea of light in the cave.
A tin tray or lid to bang and give the effect of thunder.

Merlin Plays Minstrel

Producing the Play   This play makes use of a number of the ideas which were popular in the time of Queen Elizabeth I. The musicians' gallery is used at the beginning of the play and at the end, when Merlin appears in his true shape as Wizard or Magician. The inner stage is used as the cave in which he appears disguised as a travelling minstrel to the boy, Arthur (later to be the famous King of Britain). Merlin makes the boy Arthur dream the story he tells, which is acted on the main stage and the first gallery. The tower which is built and then collapses is operated through the central trapdoor. This is later used for the appearance of the Red and White Dragons.

An important point to remember is that in any theatre *right* is always the actor's *right*, and *left* is the actor's *left*, looking towards the audience.

SCENE ONE

At the beginning of the play put out the flag. Blow an imaginary trumpet. Merlin, as Magician, appears on musicians' gallery. Make sound of thunder.

MERLIN (*ghostly voice, as if from far away*): Arthur. Merlin calls you.

ARTHUR (*appearing through trapdoor down-stage right*): I thought I heard someone calling. How can it be? I don't see anyone. This is a lonely place; I've never been here before.

MERLIN (*a little louder*): Arthur. Arthur. Merlin calls you.

ARTHUR: It's very strange. I see no one but I keep hearing my name. (*Move Arthur along track towards inner stage.*)

MERLIN: Arthur! Arthur! Hear the voice of Merlin, Merlin the Magician.

ARTHUR: A strange feeling urges me forward. I run. I jump.

MERLIN (*softly*): Ah. My spell is beginning to work. He hears me.

ARTHUR: Oh, I am hot and thirsty. Here's a stream, now if only I were a fish, swimming, floating.

MERLIN: Arthur! Arthur!

ARTHUR: Perhaps I could fly like a bird. But I am high up in the mountains now. This is where the stream starts. I think I'll have a rest here in this cave in the rocks. (*He goes through curtains to inner stage.*)

MERLIN (*speaking with great power*):
There is the boy who one day I will bring
To his future role as Britain's greatest King.
It is too soon for him to know me now,
But he must hear of Merlin's power.
I will pretend to be a Minstrel who has lost his way,
One who sings songs of a bygone day.

13

Thus will I teach him Merlin's name
And my everlasting fame. (*Exit*)
(*When Merlin as Minstrel and Arthur are in position, roll up curtains of inner stage; it is lined with silver paper to make it gleam.*)

ARTHUR: What a queer place. Light from above makes the rocks gleam and shine. I feel quite lost. Where am I? Who are you?

MINSTREL: If you are lost, boy, so am I.

ARTHUR: I thought I heard someone calling my name.

MINSTREL: Perhaps you heard me singing to keep up my spirits.

ARTHUR: It's very odd round here. Do you feel it? You haven't said who you are.

MINSTREL: I am a minstrel on my way to Court.

ARTHUR: Court? But that's a long way off.

MINSTREL: Then I have a long journey ahead. Perhaps you can help me to find my way out of this wood.

ARTHUR (*sleepily*): Let me rest a little first and then perhaps I'll remember better how I came. Can you not sing some more?

MINSTREL: I came here searching for the place where King Vortigern first met Merlin, the Magician.

ARTHUR (*still sleepy*): Who's Merlin?

MINSTREL: Magician, Doctor, Wizard, all of these. He is skilled in every art. The King makes no important decision without his help.

ARTHUR: He must be clever. Tell me more.

MINSTREL (*half singing*):
High in these mountains near a cave and spring,
Merlin first proved his power to the King,
Where the great rock split in two,
And the light came shining through.

Merlin as a minstrel   *Arthur as a boy*   *Merlin as a boy*

ARTHUR: That might have been a cave like this one.
MINSTREL: Yes, near just such a cave as this one
The King was building a tower, to defend his kingdom . . .
ARTHUR *(very sleepily)*: Tell on. . . .
MINSTREL: Each day the builders worked with all their might,
And yet the tower fell down every night . . .
Ah, the boy's asleep. Now let him dream the rest.
(Lower curtain on cave. Raise King Vortigern's tower through the central trapdoor. Place procession of workmen on cotton-reel rollers, left. The King and his Adviser appear on first gallery. Downstage right Merlin as Boy appears with his hands behind his back as if tied. A guard is behind him. By turning cotton-reel rollers bring workmen into view, or use larger individual puppets.)

SCENE TWO

1ST WORKMAN: Silly, I call it, downright stupid. We keep on trying to build this tower, higher and higher, and then whoosh, one more lot of rock and down it comes. I don't like this job at all.
2ND WORKMAN: You're right, friend. I can't think what they're at.
1ST WORKMAN: It's those magic men. They think they know everything. One more try, one more try. Why here? Why not some place else?
2ND WORKMAN: Something to do with the stars, that's what I heard.
1ST WORKMAN: The stars had better be right this time. Every time I get near the tower I take care to move off as quickly as I can.

Workman   Workman   King Vortigern

2ND WORKMAN: I keep my fingers crossed. That's supposed to help. Look, there's the King watching us.

1ST WORKMAN: Get a move on. Get a move on. We're planning to get this tower up by sunset. (*Roll procession of workmen.*)

ADVISER: Ah, your Majesty, I see the men are working hard.

KING: The hour of danger draws near.

ADVISER: We shall not fail this time. At sunset we shall make a sacrifice. The stars have told us that this must be done.

KING: What is the sacrifice?

ADVISER: We've found a boy who looks quite human—
But 'tis not so—he is the Devil's child,
The cause of all this trouble.

KING: You are quite sure?

ADVISER: Indeed, Sire, he's been up to every trick. We found him in the kitchens, pretending to make food vanish. I told him to be off home. 'I have no home—send me off and I'll go to the Devil,' was his reply. He is the one to sacrifice.
(*Merlin as Boy, with guard behind him, comes up through trapdoor, right.*)

BOY: Let me go. Let me go. I would speak to the King.

GUARD: Fierce, aren't you, can't do much with your hands tied.

BOY: Let me go! Let me go! (*They appear to struggle.*)
I will speak to the King. I will speak to the King.

KING: Guard, bring the boy forward. (*Guard and Boy move nearer King.*)

Court Adviser   *Guard*   *Dragon (Red and White)*

BOY: Mercy, mercy. They say you will kill me.

KING: It is because the stars have told us how to save the kingdom. You are to be the sacrifice so that my tower will not fall.

BOY: But look at it, your Majesty. It will fall anyway.

KING: You cannot be right and all my wise men wrong.

BOY: I tell you it will fall again. I know. I have the sight. I can see the future. Your wise men are jealous of my power. That's why they want to kill me.

KING: But you are just a boy.

BOY: I know, but I can see things. I tell you (*his voice goes into a trance*) the tower will fall. . . .

ADVISER: Nonsense, prepare him for. . . (*Make clap of thunder.*)

BOY: And when it goes two dragons will come forth, and fight.
Two dragons, red, and white—
Red for the blood you mean to spill,
White for truth which I must tell.
(*Another clap of thunder. Operate procession of workmen.*)

WORKMEN: The tower is shaking. It's falling.

ADVISER: Kill the boy, quickly.

KING: No. Do not touch him. If his prophecy is true, I will spare him.
(*Make the tower collapse through the trapdoor. Bring up Red and White dragons who fight until White wins. They disappear.*)

KING: The prophecy was true. Guards, release this boy. Care for him as if he were a Prince. We must be advised by him.

BOY: Thank you, your Majesty.
No tower that you build will e'er be sound
While dragons fight at night beneath the ground.
The power of Britain cannot stand
While wars divide the rulers of the land.
Seek not to build a tower—it will be no defence.
Though you are great, after you will come a greater
Arthur, King of Britain.
(*Take off these characters. Re-open curtains to inner stage.*)

ARTHUR (*repeating sleepily*): Arthur, King of Britain. Arthur. He said Arthur, King of Britain. I've had the strangest dream.

MINSTREL: Come and show me the way out of this wood. I'll tell you more tales to shorten the journey.

ARTHUR: Tell me more about Merlin. What happened next?
(*They go off.*) (*Merlin as Magician appears again on musicians' gallery.*)

MERLIN: And further tales you'll hear another day
When Merlin's magic brings another play.
All future times will then record the story
Of Merlin's learning, and of Arthur's glory.

CHAPTER 2 The Punch & Judy Theatre

With some changes the Elizabethan type of theatre continued to be built for about a hundred years. Under the rule of Cromwell, however, there followed a difficult time for those people who enjoyed plays. In the Puritan England of this period, theatres were closed and the performance of plays was banned. Amusements of any sort were frowned upon.

However, one type of theatre did manage to carry on without too much trouble. That was the travelling puppet theatre. The reason it succeeded was that one or two men could put on a whole show. The theatre was a little booth which could be taken away very quickly. Later, this type of theatre developed its own popular hero, Mr. Punch.

Since Punch is only a puppet he can't really get into trouble with Authority for what he says and does, and he therefore pleases himself and the audience with his antics. His popular catch-phrase nowadays is 'That's the way to do it', usually when he is doing something quite outrageous!

If two puppeteers are putting on a Punch and Judy show, one acts as the Bottler and wears a top hat. He is called the Bottler because he collects money from the audience in a bottle. Then when everything is ready he goes behind the scenes and helps with any extra puppets and by handing things to the Punch and Judy man. But if the puppeteer gives the show alone he has to make sure that he can keep one puppet in sight and change the other characters below the opening. In a proper puppet theatre the puppets are hung on hooks but you cannot do this with a cardboard box theatre, so if you decide to give a more complicated play than the one in this book, you must work out a way to change puppets behind the table.

MAKING A PUPPET BOOTH

what you need

★ Large cutting-out scissors, pencil, ruler, colours, etc., as before.
★ A cardboard grocery carton about 40 cm by 20 cm by 20 cm.

what you do

1. Unfasten the long flaps and open out the short flaps, then stand the box on end.
2. Bend the top short flap upwards and cut into a triangle to make the top of the theatre. Use another piece of cardboard to brace the flap at the back, and fix in place with Sellotape.

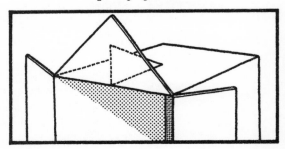

top half of carton

3. Cut off the long flaps leaving a narrow edge down each side. Turn over about 3 cm of the bottom flap to make a ledge. Cut a slit in narrow edge at either side, through which this ledge can be slotted.

4. Fasten the bottom flap securely to each side with Sellotape or paste.

5. Colour the box in the traditional stripes of the Punch and Judy theatre.

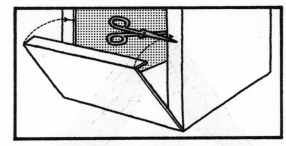

bottom half of carton

PUNCH AND TOBY

MAKING THE PUPPETS

what you need

★ An old pair of stockings, tights, or socks, ready to be thrown away.

★ A plastic spoon; a hair-roller; a clothes-peg.

★ Needle and cotton; paper-clips.

★ Paints, crayons, scissors, paper, etc.

★ Colourful scraps of material for making Punch's hat and Toby's ruff and tail. Stiff material for Toby's ears.

what you do

For the three puppets in the play that follows, we are using three different types of puppet head:

(A) plastic spoon head with mask for the BULL

1. Cut a piece of stocking or sock long enough to cover your hand and go half-way up to your elbow. (Keep the foot-part for use later.)

2. Sew the neck of the spoon firmly in position in the centre of the stocking piece.

Oversew from each side of the spoon to the corners of the stocking.

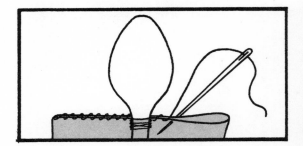

20

3. On folded paper draw the Bull mask face as in the diagram.
4. Cut out, leaving the tops of the ears joined.
5. Colour in the Bull's face and head.

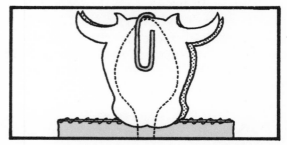

6. Paper-clip the back of the mask to the plastic spoon.
    You act this puppet with your hand inside the piece of stocking and your forefinger and thumb holding the spoon.

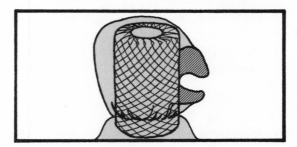

(B) hair-roller puppet for PUNCH

1. Take the stocking foot and put it over the hair-roller.
2. Pad inside with extra pieces of stocking until you have the shape of the head and neck. Add the big hooked nose inside with a piece of plastic foam, thin card or paper, and sew in position.
3. Gather up the end of the stocking and sew to the roller to make the neck.

4. Cut another piece of stocking for the body. Turn in the raw edges and sew the roller securely into the centre. Oversew each side to make the corners.
5. Paint or embroider the face.
6. Make the traditional Punch hat from a scrap of colourful material. Mr. Punch always has this sort of hat and a hooked nose.
    This puppet is operated with the forefinger through the hair-roller and the thumb and middle finger in the corners of the stocking body for the arms.

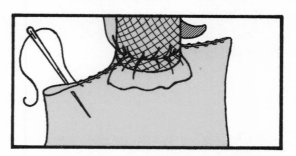

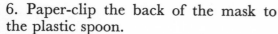

21

(C) clothes-peg puppet for TOBY THE DOG

This is a suitable puppet for a character which needs to use its mouth.

1. Take a piece of stocking which has the toe at one end.

2. Put a clothes-peg inside the toe and turn enough stocking into the open clothes-peg to cover the 'snapping jaws'.
3. Hold the peg open with a pencil and sew around upper and lower parts of peg to make 'jaws'.

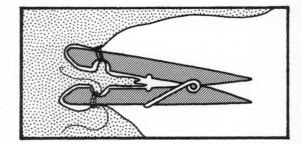

4. Cut another piece of stocking and stuff it into the head on the upper side of the clothes-peg. Gather up any slack behind the head and stitch to make the 'neck'.
5. Sew on two triangular scraps of stiff material for the ears.
6. For the ruff to go round the neck, tack a straight piece of material; gather up to the right length, then sew on.
7. Sew a strip of material on the back for a tail.

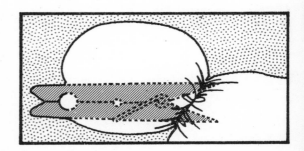

8. Make a 'doggy' face with felt pens or paints, or embroider the eyes and nose.

This puppet is operated with the thumb and forefinger holding the clothes-peg inside the stocking and working the 'jaws' as desired.

Punch and Toby

a play for the Punch and Judy Theatre

Characters

Mr. Punch
Toby, his Dog
The Bull

Properties

Punch's stick
Toby's bone
Punch's dinner plate
A baby's bottle
(All these are carried by Toby in his 'clothes-peg jaws' and can be made out of cardboard, coloured on each side.)
A piece of red cloth or red paper for Punch to wave at the Bull

Producing the play   Set up your box theatre on a table and have the puppets and properties ready beforehand in a convenient place. Wear a dark shirt or jersey so that you will not be so noticeable behind the theatre. When you are ready to begin, bring Mr. Punch up in the opening of the booth. If people are still talking, make him speak very loudly and keep calling for attention until everyone is settled.

PUNCH	(*poking head out of booth*): That's right. Step this way. Just over here. Come and see Punch and Toby, Punch and Toby. That's the way to do it. Fooled you, didn't I? Punch and Toby today, not Punch and Judy. Over here, Madam, just the place for you. On the floor with the kiddies. That's the way to do it. Don't push. Stop gabbing. When you're ready. Are you ready? (*Wait for an answer.*)
AUDIENCE:	Yes!
PUNCH	(*continues if audience says nothing*): I said, are you ready? You're supposed to say 'Yes'. Say 'Yes'.
AUDIENCE:	Yes!
PUNCH:	Can't you speak up?
AUDIENCE	(*louder, we hope!*): YES!
PUNCH:	That's the way to do it. Judy! Judy! Where's that stupid woman? Judy! Oh, wait a minute, she's gone out. That's the way to do it. Taken the baby to see Grannie. Ha! Ha! That'll be fun for them. Left me on my own.
TOBY	(*putting head up*): Arf. Arf! Arf. Arf! Arf!
PUNCH:	Oh, except for you, Toby. That's right—you're doing the show with me today. Punch and Toby we'll call it. That's the way to do it. Come on now, show the people how clever you are. Are you going to do the show with me? One bark is 'No'. Two barks for 'Yes'.

TOBY	(*one bark*) : Arf!
PUNCH:	Come on, come on—that's not the answer.
TOBY:	Arf!
PUNCH:	What's that, silly? One bark or two? 'No' or 'Yes'?
TOBY:	Arf. Arf!
PUNCH:	Good dog! Good dog! Just like a circus dog, that's what you are. Now show off your tricks. Fetch my stick. (*Toby goes off and comes back with Punch's stick.*) Come on now! Good boy! Fetch it here! Fetch! Fetch! (*Toby stays just out of reach.*) Oh you are a nuisance! Give it to me! Come on, give it to me! (*Punch turns to the audience and raises his arms in despair.*)
TOBY:	Arf! Arf! (*He hits Punch with the stick from behind.*)
PUNCH	(*swinging round and grabbing*) : That's NOT the way to do it. (*He pulls on the stick and they have a tug-of-war until Toby lets go suddenly and Punch falls backward, but he has the stick.*)
PUNCH:	I'll show you, you silly little dog. (*He raises the stick.*)
TOBY:	Arf!
PUNCH:	All right, but try harder this time. Now sit.
TOBY:	Arf! Arf! (*But he runs round as if he is chasing his tail.*)
PUNCH:	I said, 'Sit', you idiot!
TOBY:	Arf! Arf! (*But he still chases his tail.*)
PUNCH:	All right then, chase your tail. (*Toby sits.*) That's the way to do it. (*You can carry on in this way for one or two other doggy tricks in which Toby turns the tables on Mr. Punch, then continue the play.*)
PUNCH:	Well, that's enough today—you need more practice. I think I'll have my dinner now. You can fetch that. (*Toby goes away and comes back with a bone.*) Not *your* dinner, fool, my dinner. (*Toby puts down the bone on the edge of the opening and comes back with the plate. He pretends to offer it to Punch and then snatches it away.*) Oh, so you think you'll try that again. We'll see. I'll have the bone. (*Punch reaches for the bone.*)
TOBY:	Grrrrr! Grrrrr! (*He holds the plate for Punch, who takes it, then Toby picks up his bone. They both pretend to eat.*)
PUNCH:	Mmm! Dee-licious. Only one thing wrong—there isn't enough. Now let me see, what would I be doing if Judy was home? I'd be rocking the baby, that's what. (*Toby goes off with the bone. Punch throws his plate away.*) Anyway that's easier than washing up. That's the way to do it. (*Toby comes back with the baby's bottle.*) Oh, you big baby! There, there, who's a woozums? Oy, I don't think Judy would like it at all if you had the baby's milk. I'll have it. (*He takes the milk bottle from Toby.*)
TOBY:	Arf! Arf!

24

PUNCH: Where shall I put it to keep it safe? Let me see, over here perhaps? (*He turns away from Toby and starts to put bottle down. Toby tries to come round behind him.*)

TOBY: Arf! Arf! Arf!

PUNCH: Oh no you don't. This milk is not for you. Think how you'd look. (*Sings*) Rock-a-bye Toby, on the tree-top, when the wind blows, the cradle will rock. I know how to keep this milk safe. I'll drink it myself.

PUNCH (*pretending to drink milk*): I didn't know babies were so lucky. There, that takes care of that. Oh, what will Judy say?

TOBY: Arf. Arf! Arf. Arf! (*He pulls at Punch's arm.*)

PUNCH: I know. Go and find a cow. Go on, Toby. I'll have a rest. (*Make snoring noise. If you are on your own, use Toby to take hold of the Bull puppet by its spoon handle. Keep Toby hidden.*)

BULL (*appearing in opening*): ARRRRR! ARRRRRR!

PUNCH: My goodness, what's that? That's not a cow! (*jumping up in a fright*) It's a bull! I need something red. (*He reaches down and gets the red cloth.*) This way! This way! Toreador, that's what I am! That's the way to do it. (*Punch waves the red flag and the Bull keeps charging at it.*) That's the way to do it. (*Finally the Bull charges off and Punch sits down exhausted.*) Whew, what a lot of work, and no milk!
(*Toby returns with the milk bottle in his mouth.*)
Oh good dog, good dog! Safely back before Judy is home! I don't think I'll put you in the circus after all. You'd rather stay with me, wouldn't you?

TOBY: Arf!

PUNCH: What was that?

TOBY: Arf! Arf!

PUNCH: That's the way to do it. Goodbye everyone!

THE END

CHAPTER 3 The Picture-Frame Theatre

After Charles II came to the throne in 1660, theatres again became the fashion. At times the plays were a little too daring, so many ladies and gentlemen, in order not to be recognised in the audience, wore masks to attend. Some members of the audience were allowed to sit on the stage itself and they began to interrupt and spoil the play for the rest. As a result there was a gradual change in the way plays were produced. The small inner stage with the curtains was used more and more, and it became larger. Then a new arch was required for the curtains which were now big and heavy. As the scenery became more complicated, so more light was needed to show up costumes and actors' movements. In this way the sort of stage we know best today came into being, with curtains and footlights. The arch at the front of the stage in grand theatres was like a huge picture-frame; it was called the *proscenium*. The orchestra was placed between the stage and the audience, making a bigger separation between players and those who came to watch. Many of these ideas had already been tried out in Italy and France so it wasn't long before all theatres were built to this pattern.

MAKING THE PICTURE-FRAME STAGE

what you need

★ Large cutting-out scissors, pencil, ruler, colours, etc., as before.
★ A cardboard grocery carton 40 cm by 25 cm by 25 cm.
★ Spare pieces of cardboard for wings and flats.
★ Three potting-rods, sticks, or straight twigs, slightly longer than the box and able to take drawing-pins.
★ Sellotape; paste; drawing-pins.
★ Clothes-pegs for holding the puppets.
★ Coloured paper for covering the picture-frame front.
★ A piece of material large enough to cover the front opening of your stage for a curtain.
★ A torch for the footlights.

what you do

1. Place the box on its long side, and unfasten the flaps. Turn all flaps outwards.
2. Paint the top and sides of the 'frame' or cover with coloured paper. Cut it in scrolls if you wish.

3. Make three holes in each side of the box at places marked **o** in the diagram. These are to hold the rods.
4. Cut out a rectangle in the top side of the box, as shown.

the curtain

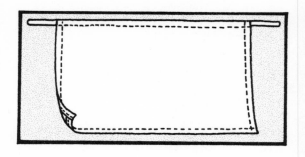

1. Turn over one long edge of the curtain material and hem, leaving enough space to push a rod through. Hem the other three sides for neatness. Insert a rod through the top hem.
2. Push one end of the rod through a front side hole, then ease the other end of the rod into the opposite side hole.
3. Drawing-pin the curtain to the rod to hold it firmly at the top. The curtain can now be rolled up and down.

the scenery

1. Put the second and third rods in position as shown. The back rod can be used to hold scenery in place or as a backcloth roller. It will also serve for fixing the top flap of the picture-frame.

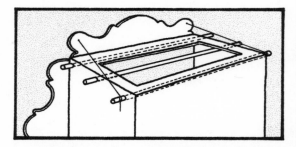

2. Tie strong thread at each corner of the top flap and secure the threads to either side of the back rod.
3. The middle rod is used for a support and a place to hook the mini marionettes.

flats and wings

This type of stage also needs flats and wings made out of cardboard.

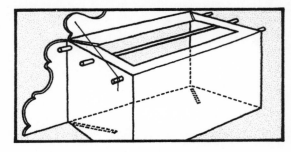

1. Make two slits about 10 cm deep in the 'ceiling' of the theatre behind the top flap. Cut at an angle as in the diagram.
2. Make two similar slits in the floor of the stage.
3. Cut two strips of cardboard a little deeper than the height of the theatre and the same width as the slits. The wings can now be fixed in position.

4. Behind the wings you should have a pair of flats which can be made by taking a piece of cardboard the height of the theatre and folding it in half.

5. Open out at an angle and fix in position between the middle and back rods.

The scenes for the wings and flats should be painted on separate pieces of paper and then clipped in place when required.

lighting

The picture-frame stage was lighted artificially from above and also by foot-lights directed towards the actors' faces.

To provide footlights for your table-top stage you can use the bottom flap at the front of the stage. Bend it in half so that you can slide a torch underneath and make a rectangular hole for the light to shine through. For coloured lighting, paint a strip of paper both sides with squares of blue, green, red and yellow, and secure the strip across the rectangular opening. If you prefer a bright white light, leave the rectangle open.

MAKING THE MINI MARIONETTES

Marionettes are puppets on strings. Some can be extremely complicated but ours are very simple because they have to be small, and obviously their movements are limited. You can if you like make them from cardboard and thread, and dangle them on the stage. To 'act' them, however, it is better to make them as little dolls with movable heads, jointed bodies, and weighted feet. This is the type we shall describe.

what you need

★ Large cutting-out scissors, pencil, ruler, colours, etc., as before.
★ Drinking-straws, or hollow, dried flower stalks.
★ Two needles and cotton.
★ Four small buttons for each puppet, if possible pairs of buttons.
★ Dough for modelling heads; this is made from a tablespoon of flour, a pinch of salt and a little water.
★ Fuse-wire or thick thread for the main control of the marionettes; fuse-wire is easier to handle.

what you do

marionette heads

1. To make the dough for the heads, put a tablespoon of flour and a pinch of salt in a saucer. Add a little water, a teaspoon at a time, and mix well. The dough should be soft enough to shape but *not* wet enough to stick to your fingers. It will harden into heads that should last a long time. Make your puppet heads about the size of marbles.

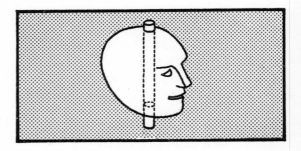

2. Stick a piece of straw about 2 cm long through each head vertically.
3. Shape the faces and the hair styles, while the dough is soft, with a pin. You will want slightly different heads for each character.
4. Leave in a warm place to harden —a day or longer—before painting or colouring with felt pens.

marionette bodies

For each puppet you need three pieces of straw 3 cm long and two pieces of straw 2 cm long.

30

1. Thread a needle with double cotton. Tie the two ends through the two holes in button, as shown. This makes your first 'foot'.

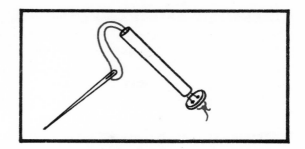

2. Push the needle through one of the long pieces of straw to add a 'leg'.

3. Thread the second needle and secure another button as before. Push this needle through another long piece of straw to make a second 'leg'. Now take both needles through the third long straw to make a 'body'.

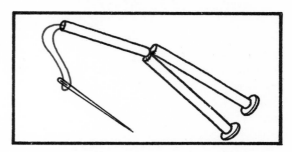

4. Take one needle through a short piece of straw for an 'arm' and fasten off with a button. Do not pull too tight as you want your arms and legs to move.
5. Make a second 'arm' in the same way. Leave ends of threads for operating the arms if desired. Cut off needles.

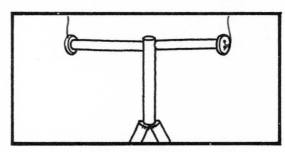

adding heads and control strings

1. The heads are attached to the bodies with fine wire. For each puppet you will need a piece long enough to stretch from the cross-bar to the floor of the stage. Push the wire up through the body of the puppet and then through the head.
2. Fasten the lower end of the wire by hooking it up the outside of the body.
3. Bend the top of the wire to hook over the cross-bar, making sure that the feet of the puppet just touch the stage. Separate control threads for arms and legs should be tied to the wire hook, when not in use.
4. To keep the head from slipping round, push a short length of flower stalk or pipe-cleaner into the head-straw and neck.

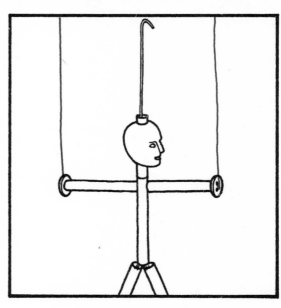

31

DRESSING THE PUPPETS

For their costumes you need bits of ribbon, gift-wrapping paper, scraps of material left from home-dressmaking, milk-bottle tops, silver foil, etc.

To fasten the materials to the puppets, use thread, glue, or Sellotape. Choose material to suit each character—rich and gaudy, or poor and simple.

A DOCTOR IN SPITE OF HIMSELF

Sganarelle (Sga-na-rell), the wood-cutter

Remember that it is the effect you are after so that the audience can tell one character from another. Sganarelle, although a woodcutter, dresses as a doctor. He is recognised by a long black coat and a scholar's hat. The hat can be kept out of sight and up the control thread until the second act.

Martine, a peasant woman, Sganarelle's wife

Shabby material cut into strips will look like rags.

Luke, a serving-man in livery

A bit of foil round the body will make a jerkin. Breeches can be made from milk-bottle tops cut in half and wrapped round legs.

Lucinda, a grand lady and the Count's daughter

For a lady's costume make a full skirt by gathering a piece of ribbon or a straight piece of rich material. Lace or other material can be draped round the shoulders.

The Count Geronte, a rich man

Take a piece of velvet ribbon twice the length of the marionette. Make a slit in the centre for the neck opening. Tie the ribbon firmly round the waist with cotton or coloured string.

Leander, a young man, in love with Lucinda

Use another piece of ribbon and the same method for making a shorter tunic. Cut milk-bottle tops in half and wrap round the upper legs for breeches.

Sganarelle, the woodcutter

Lucinda, a grand lady

Martine, a peasant woman

Luke, a serving man

Count Geronte

Leander

33

A Doctor in Spite of Himself

Adapted for the Picture-frame theatre from the French play by Molière

Producing the Play The first scene can be played in the forward half of the stage. This scene takes place outside Sganarelle's hut. The hut is painted on paper and clipped on the double flat which divides the stage. Paint big trees to clip on the wings at either side. You will also need to paint scenery for the Count's drawing-room and the entrance hall. The drawing-room can be clipped in position over the back rod with clothes-pegs. The entrance hall can be painted to go on the double flat after the first scene is taken away.

ACT ONE

(The curtain rises on Sganarelle, the woodcutter, who is dressed in his doctor's gown. He is quarrelling with Martine, his wife.)

MARTINE: Just look at you! Never was a man more ridiculous, flapping about like a crow in the old gown your master gave you.

SGANARELLE: And why not? He was a rich doctor. It's well made.

MARTINE: It's not much use to you now you chop wood for a living.

SGANARELLE: It's all I have.

MARTINE: Whose fault is that? Oh, why did I ever marry you? I might have guessed you would eat up all I owned.

SGANARELLE: You're wrong; I drank most of it.

MARTINE: That's all your late master taught you; how to drink.

SGANARELLE: Wrong again. He taught me Latin.

MARTINE: Latin! Language of fools!

SGANARELLE: Don't shout. You give me a headache.

MARTINE: I'll shout if I want to; I have some rights. Rogue, cheat, drunkard. . . .

SGANARELLE *(starting to chase her)*: I warned you.

MARTINE *(screaming as she flops down on the stage)*: Oh-i-ee. Leave me alone.

SGANARELLE: Oh women! You shouldn't take on so. What's a little quarrel between husband and wife?

MARTINE: You're a hard-hearted brute.

SGANARELLE: Oh I'm off. I'll go to work to get a little peace. *(Exit.)*

MARTINE: Work, I don't believe. He's got a bottle hidden somewhere. I'll get even with him, somehow.
(Enter Luke.)

LUKE: I seem to have lost my way. There's no use looking for a doctor here at the edge of the forest.

MARTINE *(rising and making a curtsey)*: May I help you, sir?

LUKE: I am searching for a doctor who can cure the Count's daughter, but I fear I have come too far into the country.

MARTINE: The Count's daughter is ill?

LUKE: Alas, yes. She has lost her speech. It is very sad since she was about to be married. My master has tried every doctor he knows but none has been able to help. He has sent me now to find a doctor who speaks Latin. He is convinced that one who speaks Latin will succeed where others have failed.

MARTINE (*who obviously has an idea*): Oh, is that so?

LUKE: But I waste your time. I am not likely to find such a man here.

MARTINE (*quickly*): You are wrong there, sir. You could not have come to a better place. In this very spot we have a man who can work remarkable cures.

LUKE: Here, in the forest?

MARTINE: Yes, here. He is a quite extraordinary man. He is a brilliant doctor but he will never exercise his talents unless he is *forced* to do so. He spends his time chopping wood, or drinking.

LUKE: That is very strange. Who is this man?

MARTINE: His name is Sganarelle. You will find him in the clearing.

LUKE: You are sure he can cure my mistress?

MARTINE: I am more than sure. A few months ago a lady was given up for dead—he had but to put a few drops of something on her tongue and she leapt to her feet and danced round the room.

LUKE: That sounds just what we require.

MARTINE: Remember that you must threaten him, even take him away and have him beaten. A good beating always works.

LUKE: I take the point. Thank you, madam. (*Exit Luke.*)

MARTINE: That will serve Sganarelle right; a good beating is just what he needs.

(*The curtain falls.*)

ACT TWO

Scene 1

(*The Count's drawing-room. Lucinda is posed on a sofa and the Count is standing mid-stage. Sganarelle enters.*)

COUNT (*to Lucinda*): I hope this doctor that Luke has found will be able to cure you. Your marriage has been put off long enough. Forget this poor chap Leander. I know that he has a rich uncle, but the uncle may live a long time. The man I have chosen for you is rich *now*. That is what matters. Ah, sir, here you are. I am indeed happy to see you. (*He bows. Sganarelle bows in reply.*)

SGANARELLE: Is this the patient then? What is wrong, Mademoiselle?

LUCINDA (*makes a mumbling noise*): Han, hi, hon, han.

SGANARELLE: What was that?

LUCINDA: Han, hi, hon, han.

SGANARELLE: Han, hi, hon, han. I have never heard this language. What on earth is she talking about?

COUNT: Sir, it is her illness. She cannot speak. It is for this we have had to postpone her marriage. The man she is to marry will not wed her until she is cured.

SGANARELLE: And who is this fool who will not marry a wife who cannot speak? Mine talks too much.

COUNT: I pray you, Sir, not to joke. Use your powers to cure her.

SGANARELLE: Let me see. Let me see. I must take your pulse. (*He bends over Lucinda.*) Mmmm!

COUNT: What do you think?

SGANARELLE: The pulse—er—indicates—er—uh—that she cannot speak.

COUNT: How clever you are—that is indeed her illness—but what causes it?

SGANARELLE: Do you speak Latin?

COUNT: No, alas, I do not.

SGANARELLE (*rattles off some Latin words*): *Quis, quis, quid, bonus, bona, bonum.*

COUNT: And what does that mean?

SGANARELLE: I think she should go to bed and have some bread soaked in wine. Good day, Sir. (*Sganarelle starts to leave the stage.*)

COUNT: Thank you, Sir, but wait for a moment.

SGANARELLE (*nervously*): Er, why?

COUNT: I wish to give you some money.

SGANARELLE: Ah, Sir, thank-you.
(*The curtain falls.*)

Scene 2
(*Put into position the double flat showing the entrance hall of the Count's house. As the curtain rises, Sganarelle moves across from left to meet Leander coming from right.*)

SGANARELLE (*to himself*): I am completely confused—first I am forced to promise I will cure the Count's daughter to avoid being beaten. Now I am paid before I have cured her. And there will be more money if I can cure her. I shall come again.

LEANDER (*approaching*): I am the only one who can cure Lucinda.

SGANARELLE: Who are you?

LEANDER: I am Leander and I *love* Lucinda. It is because her father will not let me see her that she has lost her speech.

SGANARELLE: You are the man she is to marry?

LEANDER: No. I am too poor. Her father will not permit this—he has another husband in mind.

SGANARELLE: But if you see her, then she will speak?

LEANDER: Yes, I am the only one who can cure her. Let me come with you as your apothecary for your next visit. Don't worry. Her father will not recognise me.

SGANARELLE: Arranged. Be here tomorrow at three o'clock.
(*The curtain falls.*)

ACT THREE

(The Count's drawing-room. Lucinda is again on the sofa. The Count is up-stage left. As the curtain rises Sganarelle, followed by Leander, enters right.)

COUNT: Ah, Sir, I was wondering when you would come again.

SGANARELLE: I have brought my apothecary with me to give your daughter some medicine which I want her to have. But may I just have a word with you here . . . *(He draws the Count aside while Leander hurries to the sofa and kneels beside Lucinda.)*

COUNT: Of course, Sir. What is it you wished to speak about?

SGANARELLE: I wish to ask your opinion on which sort of patient you feel is the most difficult to treat, a man or a woman. Now in my opinion . . .

LUCINDA *(loudly)*: No. I insist. I will not change my mind.

COUNT: My daughter speaks. You have cured her. Oh, I am obliged to you, Sir.

LUCINDA: Yes, Father, I have recovered my speech but it is only to say that I will never marry anybody but Leander.

COUNT: But . . .

LUCINDA: Nothing will make me change my mind. It is useless for you to suggest anything else . . .

COUNT: What?

LUCINDA: I am not going to change my mind.

COUNT: If . . .

LUCINDA: All your speeches will waste your breath.

COUNT: I . . .

LUCINDA: I am quite determined.

COUNT: But . . .

LUCINDA: Nothing is going to make me marry against my will.

COUNT: I have . . .

LUCINDA: You have spoken in vain.

COUNT: He . . .

LUCINDA: No. My heart will not submit to your tyranny.

COUNT: The . . .

LUCINDA: I'll go to a convent rather than marry a man I don't love.

COUNT: But . . .

LUCINDA: You're wasting time. I've made up my mind.

COUNT: My, what a flow of speech. Sir, I pray you, make her mute again.

SGANARELLE: That's impossible. All I can do is make you deaf.

COUNT: Thank you very much. *(To Lucinda)* What do you think?

LUCINDA: It's no use asking me. I'm not going to change.

COUNT: You'll do as you are told.

LUCINDA: I'd rather marry a corpse.

SGANARELLE: Listen to me. Our apothecary will cure this. The name in Latin for the cure is *matrimonium cum tuum* as soon as possible. Understand, Mr. Apothecary?

LEANDER: Yes, Sir.

(Leander and Lucinda go off together.)

COUNT: What is this drug, *matrimonium?*

SGANARELLE: Girls are sometimes difficult and in certain cases medicines like these are urgent necessities.

(Enter Luke.)

LUKE: Sir, your daughter has run off with Leander, whom *he (looks at Sganarelle)* has introduced as an apothecary.

COUNT: What? To treat me in such a fashion. Go at once for a magistrate, quickly, quickly. Oh, you traitor, I will have you punished.

(Exit Luke. Enter Martine.)

MARTINE: Oh my goodness, what a time I have had finding this place. *(To the Count)* Tell me, Sir, have you seen a doctor hereabouts?

COUNT: There he is. He will probably be hanged.

MARTINE: What? Hanged? What has he done?

COUNT: He has helped my daughter to elope against my will.

MARTINE *(going to Sganarelle)*: What, my poor husband, is it really true?

SGANARELLE: You see what has happened. What can I do?

COUNT: When the magistrate comes, I will see you are put in prison for your crime!

(Enter Leander and Lucinda.)

LEANDER: Sir, I have come to return Lucinda to your house. We did intend to elope and get married but it was not honourable. I only wish to receive Lucinda's hand from you. That which I must tell you, Sir, is that I am no longer penniless. My uncle has died and left me all his property. I am a rich man.

COUNT: Sir, I see you with joy. You are a man to be respected. I give you the hand of my daughter with the blessing you deserve.

SGANARELLE: Thank heavens the medicine has worked.

MARTINE: You will not now be hanged so you might do me the honour of remaining a doctor since I have done this for you.

SGANARELLE: You might have had me beaten or hanged!

LEANDER: But she did not and the end result is more than worth your while.

SGANARELLE: True. I pardon you, my dear wife, but you must treat me with proper respect—and—remember that the anger of a doctor can be greater even than that of a woodcutter!

THE CURTAIN FALLS

CHAPTER 4   The Open Stage

In recent years the open or arena stage, with the audience sitting round three sides, has again come into fashion. The modern theatre uses cleverly designed sets on different levels with very little formal scenery or furniture. In this respect it looks back to the theatre of Shakespeare's day. The difference is that it has all the advantages of up-to-date lighting equipment and electrical machinery; this made it possible to do away with the heavy curtains and the archway which divided the players from the audience for three hundred years.

Our play, 'Dive to Danger', makes particular use of lighting effects and suggests ways in which you can construct them safely for a tabletop theatre.

MAKING THE OPEN STAGE

what you need

★ A cardboard grocery carton about 40 cm by 30 cm by 20 cm.

what you do

1. Place the box open side down on your working surface.

2. Cut out a rectangular section large enough to put your hand and arm through.

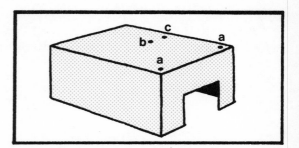

3. Make small holes on the top of the box where indicated in the diagram:

a rod holes for the back-cloth

b a hole for the turntable stage

c a hole for the lighting gantry.

4. Cut out a strip about 15 cm by 5 cm near the front of the stage.

5. Cut a rectangle for the trapdoor. It should be large enough to push the sea monster through.

MAKING THE TURNTABLE STAGE

what you need

★ An empty cotton reel.

★ A piece of rod or stick, pencil-length, that will fit into the centre of the cotton reel to make a handle.

★ A circular piece of cardboard about 10 cm in diameter.

★ Small cardboard boxes or children's bricks on which to raise and lower the turntable stage.

★ Drawing-pins; paste.

what you do

1. Wedge the pencil-length stick into the cotton reel. If necessary secure it with paste or glue.

2. Fix the cardboard circle to the top of the cotton reel with paste and drawing-pins.

3. Push the other end of the stick through hole **b** in the floor of the main stage.

By operating the handle from underneath you can raise, lower, and turn this stage to different positions. Use boxes or bricks to make the final position firm.

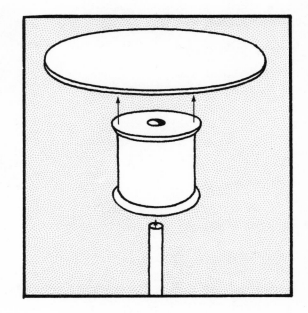

MAKING THE STAGE MACHINERY
the back-cloth

what you need

★ Three knitting-needles or potting-rods.
★ A needle and cotton.
★ A piece of plain thin material.
★ Paints or felt pens.
★ Silver foil to give shimmering effect.

what you do

1. Use paint or felt pens to make the material rainbow-coloured. Start at the top with red, then yellow and green, and end with a blue which gets darker and darker as it reaches the bottom.

2. Hem the sides of the material, leaving enough space to insert a rod across the top and the two rods at the sides for uprights.

3. When the back-cloth is completed, push the upright rods into the two holes at **a** on the stage.

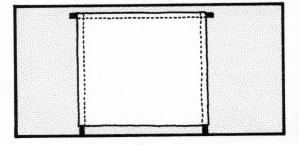

41

the lighting gantry

what you need

★ A plastic carton.
★ A small torch.
★ An empty cotton reel.
★ A pencil-sized stick for the handle.
★ Drawing-pins; a needle with a big eye; thin string or strong cotton.

what you do

1. Cut a circle out of the base of the carton so that the torch can shine through.
2. With the needle make four holes at the places marked **x**. Thread the cotton or string through the holes.
3. Attach the carton firmly to the top of the cotton reel with drawing-pins. Tie the torch in position in the carton.
4. Push the pencil-sized stick into the cotton reel for the handle and place in the hole marked **c** on the stage. You can now raise, lower and turn the light as for the turntable stage.

DIVE TO DANGER

MAKING MAGNETIC PUPPETS

what you need

★ Paper, colouring materials.
★ A magnet.
★ About six steel pins for each puppet.

what you do

1. Cover the cut-out strip across the front of the stage with a piece of paper, and paste down with an overlap at the sides. Paint or colour the strip to suit the play.
2. Cut out the paper puppets as shown for the rod puppets on p. 11. Paint or colour.

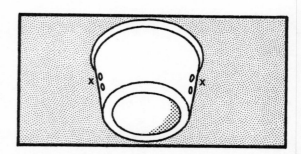

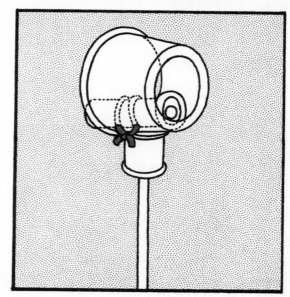

3. Instead of rods, use several steel pins through the base of each puppet.

4. The puppets can be made to move from inside the box by using the magnet *underneath* the strip of paper.

This method is very suitable for puppets like the fish and the sea creatures in this play.

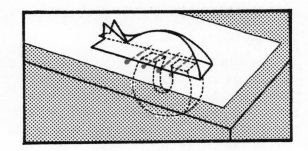

MAKING PIPE-CLEANER PUPPETS

what you need

★ At least one pipe-cleaner for each diver.

★ Cotton wool or plastic foam for heads.

★ Long strand of dark wool to wind round bodies.

★ Sellotape or cellophane for diving helmets.

★ Cotton thread or fuse-wire for controls (in this play only needed for Simon).

★ Buttons for feet so puppet can stand (for Andrew only).

what you do

1. Cut off 3 cm from a pipe-cleaner.

2. Twist the rest of the pipe-cleaner as shown. Add the short pieces to make arms.

3. Fill the head space with cotton wool, tissue or plastic foam. Draw face.

4. Fix Sellotape round the heads of both puppets for diving helmets.

5. **Andrew** Poke the pipe-cleaner 'legs' into buttons. Wind wool round and round body to make diving-suit, finishing off wool at waist.

6. **Simon** Fasten fuse-wire or cotton thread to head and waist so that he can be operated from above as a swimming diver. His legs remain free.

Andrew

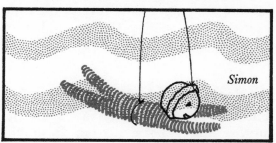

Simon

43

MAKING THE PROPERTIES

the diving-bell

1. For this you will need a plastic cup with part of the side cut out. Cover the cut-out portion with transparent packaging material fixed on with Sellotape. This is the 'window' through which the divers can be seen.

2. Fix the diving-bell to the centre of the turntable stage with drawing-pins so that it can come down with the closed side to the audience and then be turned to show the inside when it is in position.

magnetic sea-bed

Have any of the magnetic puppets you wish to use in position on the strip at the front of the stage. Goldfish are the only essential ones. String them together so that they can be pulled away quickly at the end.

the deep-sea monster

This can be made from a cardboard tube or long plastic carton. It should have a huge eye or eyes to give a menacing appearance and it can be brightly coloured. Fix a small torch inside, as for the lighting gantry.

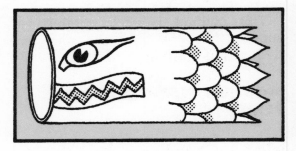

papier maché rocks

Papier maché is easy to make and excellent for modelling scenery.

Take one whole spread of newspaper. Tear it into small squares. Leave to soak overnight in two teacups of water mixed with wallpaper-paste granules. The next day scrunch it into the shapes you want and leave for several days in a warm place to dry. Paint to look like rocks.

Put the rocks on a plastic carton lid and thread a piece of cotton through. The rocks can then be pulled away easily to show the treasure chest.

the treasure chest

Use a small box and paint it to look like a treasure chest.

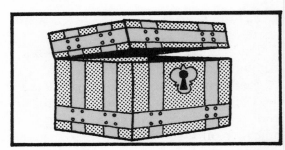

Dive to Danger

a play for the open stage

characters: *Voice from Control Ship*
(speak into glass jar or plastic carton)
Divers: *Simon Andrew*
Sea Monster
Magnetic Sea Creatures: *Any shape or type you wish—only goldfish are essential*

properties

A treasure chest
A black cord to look like an oil-rig line tangled in the treasure chest. Papier maché rocks to hide the chest
A magnet

Producing the play At the beginning of the play the diving-bell is slowly lowered on the turntable stage. You can use an empty detergent carton to blow gusts of air against the back-cloth to make it shimmer. The light should be directed towards the back-cloth and should be lowered slowly with the diving-bell.

    VOICE: Control Ship to Diving-Bell, are you receiving me? Over. (*Pause.*) Control Ship to Diving-Bell, are you receiving me? Over. (*Pause. Voice becomes more anxious.*) Control Ship to Diving-Bell, are you receiving me? Over.

    SIMON: Diving-Bell to Control. Visibility poor. Rocking.

    ANDREW: And rolling, you can tell him that too.

    SIMON: A bit more sway now.
(*Gradually move the turntable stage down towards the main stage.*)

    VOICE: Control to Diving-Bell. You are nearing sea-bed. Prepare for landing.

    SIMON: Get ready, Andrew, we're coming in to land.

    ANDREW: And bump, here we are. Phew, what a spin.
(*Bring turntable stage to final position so that the audience can see the divers in the bell.*)

    SIMON: You were right about rock and roll.
(*Turn the light to shine on to the turntable so that the diving-bell is clearly seen.*)

    SIMON (*continuing*): Diving-Bell to Control. Diving-Bell to Control.

    VOICE: Come in Diving-Bell.

    SIMON: We've landed safely.

    VOICE: Good. Have a rest before you start work. We'll call you later. Over and out.

    SIMON: Have a rest is right. What a trip!

    ANDREW: Funny, I never thought it would be like that.

    SIMON: Like what?

45

ANDREW: All those colours. It was like diving through a rainbow. And now black—whew, it is really dark out there.
(*Move magnetic fish slightly to give a shimmering effect.*)
What's that?

SIMON: What's what?

ANDREW: I thought I saw a sparkle. Like stars.

SIMON: You're dreaming. We won't see anything until we get the searchlight working.
(*Move fish again.*)

ANDREW: There it is again. Like fairy lights.

SIMON: You ought to be a poet, not a deep-sea diver. We're down here to see what could have fouled the oil-rig line, not to see fairies. We probably won't even see any fish.

ANDREW: Oh well.

SIMON: Just forget the fairy lights and have a rest. Control will be calling us soon enough. You take the first watch, and don't wake me. If you see anything, it's your imagination. I'm turning our light out. I sleep better in the dark.
(*Switch off the torch in the gantry which lights the diving-bell. Light torch in the sea monster and operate him through one of the trapdoors with his light beam pointed away from the bell. Move magnetic fish or pull on a thread to suggest that the monster is chasing them.*)

ANDREW (*in a frightened voice*): Simon. SIMON.

SIMON: Uhhh. What is it?

ANDREW: I do see a light and it's coming this way.

SIMON: Let me see. You're right, you're absolutely right. We'd better call Control. There's something down here with us.
(*Make a clicking noise.*)
Diving-Bell to Control. Diving-Bell to Control. Emergency call. Over.

ANDREW (*a little frightened*): It's coming closer.
(*Move turntable slightly.*)
Did you feel that?

SIMON (*keeping voice steady*): Diving-Bell to Control. Are you receiving me? Emergency. Over.

VOICE: Hello, Diving-Bell. Thought you were asleep. What's up?

SIMON: There's something down here with a searchlight.

VOICE (*astonished*): A searchlight?

SIMON: Yes, it's shining it all round the bell.

VOICE: You're dreaming.

ANDREW: More like a nightmare.

VOICE: Perhaps it's a reflection. Turn your light off.

SIMON: It is off. We don't dare switch it on.

VOICE: But who could it be?

46

SIMON: Someone else after our oil strike?

VOICE: Not very likely. I'd better get some advice. Just keep quite calm. Over and out.

ANDREW: Keep quite calm—ha, what else could we do?

(*Move turntable again.*)

Hey, don't rock the boat.

SIMON: Get your emergency kit ready.

ANDREW: Check.

(*Move turntable again to rock diving-bell. Then pull the last of the fish or papier maché rocks away from treasure chest and allow monster's light beam to shine on it.*)

Say, do you see what I see?

SIMON: It looks like an old sea chest.

(*Move light.*)

ANDREW: Gone.

(*Shine torch on chest again.*)

SIMON: No, there it is, and our oil line. No wonder the signals went mad.

ANDREW: What do we do now?

(*Take off monster. Pause.*)

SIMON (*in the dark*): Whatever that was, it's gone.

ANDREW: Think we should put the light on?

SIMON: Yes, let's use our own searchlight and decide what to do. I know what I'd like to do.

(*Lower lighting gantry so that torch beam will operate round the stage as a searchlight instead of focusing on the turntable stage. Switch on.*)

ANDREW: What then?

SIMON: I'm going to swim over to the chest.

ANDREW: Suppose 'they' come back.

SIMON: It's our oil line and we're here to fix it.

ANDREW: What about the chest?

SIMON: I'll see if it's worth bothering about. You keep the light steady and talk to Control.

ANDREW: Aren't you going to wait for their O.K?

SIMON: No. I might miss my chance. I'll just pressurize my diving-suit and go out through the safety hatch.

(*Blow a few times on the detergent tube to make a sound like air pressure. Then move Simon upwards in jerks, using both strings to make him 'swim' round the diving-bell and over to the chest, downstage right. When he speaks now, use a plastic cup or glass jar.*)

SIMON: I've switched on my inter-com. Can you hear me?

ANDREW: Yes, I hear you.

SIMON: Brr! It's cold out here. I'll keep moving. Shift the light a bit so I can see. That's luck. It's not too badly tangled.

47

VOICE: Control to Diving-Bell. Control to Diving-Bell. Are you receiving? Over.

ANDREW: Diving-Bell to Control. Receiving loud and clear.

VOICE: What's happened? We can hear Simon on our talkback.

ANDREW: The strange light disappeared so he went to clear the oil line.

VOICE: Switch over so I can talk to him.

SIMON: I can hear you. I've fixed the line now if you want to check it.

VOICE: Good work. Swim clear while we check.

(Make a grinding noise and move the black cord on the floor of stage.)
That's all right. You can come back up. Glad you've stopped seeing things. Over and out.

ANDREW: I've switched them off, Simon. What about the chest?

SIMON: I'm just going to have a look.

(As Simon bends over the sea chest, make a splashing noise by crumpling some paper.)
Well, I never thought . . .
(Switch on sea monster light.)

ANDREW: Come away quick—there's the light again.

SIMON: I'll keep out of the beam.

ANDREW: You'd better be quick.

SIMON: Keep him busy. Head him off with our light.

(Stage a battle with the monster's light crossing the light from the gantry, and have Simon bobbing about trying to keep out of the beams.)

ANDREW: Where are you? I think he's coming this way.

SIMON: Flash the beam towards the sea chest and I'll swim above it.

ANDREW: If only something would head him off.

SIMON: I'm right over him now; I'll just try. . . .

(Make a great splashing noise.)
That'll keep him for a minute. I'm coming in on the beam.
(While the monster twists and turns, let Simon follow the light back to the diving-bell.)

ANDREW: I'm glad you made it. This thing is rocking like mad.

SIMON: Seal the hatch. We'd better get away.

ANDREW: Right!

(Start the diving-bell upwards and bring the lighting gantry up as well. Monster twists and turns, then stops. Switch off its torch.)

SIMON: I wish I'd had a better look. All I could do was twist his tail.

ANDREW: What was it, do you think?

SIMON: I don't suppose we'll ever know—some giant electric-ray fish, I expect.

ANDREW: Maybe it was a Sea Monster. What was in the chest?

SIMON: You'll never believe it—a whole lot of goldfish.

(End play with torch shining on fish 'swimming' out of chest.)

48   **THE END**